IT Service-Continuity Management 101

Paul Edward Love MSc

Paul E. Love 2015

Notice of Liability
While every precaution has been taken in the preparation
of this book, neither the author nor the publisher shall
have any liability to any person or entity with respect to
any loss or damage caused or alleged to be caused directly
or indirectly by the instructions contained in this book or
by the products described in it.

Contents

Introduction

What is IT Service-Continuity Management?

Disaster Recovery was once considered a luxury. After all why plan for something that won't happen to us? This perception has eroded over time as more and more companies began realizing that, yes, things can go wrong, and incidents and events can seriously damage their business and brand—or, worse, take the company down. With that realization came an awareness of risk and risk management throughout the IT industry. As a result, risk mitigation emerged, just as corporate businesses began relying heavily on technology. It's an IT problem; therefore, IT can fix it.

Actually, IT service-continuity management and disaster recovery is a subset of business-continuity management.

Business continuity refers to the continuity of a business function or process in the absence of a critical resource, such as computing, office space, people, telephone, electricity, utilities, hardcopy mail, hardcopy records, legal documents/contracts, and so on. This is also known as business-continuity planning.

In an ideal world, a **Business-Continuity Plan (BCP)** should be developed and maintained by each business unit and should address how a critical business function will maintain operations, protect its assets, and effectively continue to conduct business should any critical resource (required by the business to effectively operate) become unavailable for a prolonged period.

IT disaster-recovery planning, or IT service-continuity management, is where

> an **IT Disaster-Recovery (DR) Plan** should support a worst-case disaster scenario (e.g., the entire site/location is projected to be inaccessible or inoperable).

A location activates the plan based on a projection that the production site will be inoperable or inaccessible for an extended period, such as seventy-two hours or longer (up to weeks or months). An IT-DR plan is one component of a comprehensive business-continuity plan (BCP).

A disaster is any event that prevents the business from continuing its usual operations at the standard work location for more than a predefined period, which is commonly known as the maximum acceptable outage (MAO) period (another acronym but not one you need to memorize).

Note: IT service continuity is holistic; it covers disaster-recovery planning and high availability. Although high availability is not disaster recovery, it can facilitate a less painful recovery in a disaster-recovery situation.

Recovery Triangle

Because IT service is impacted, IT service continuity is maintained by the provision of high-availability technologies. This first parachute catches the component-failure incident, which could normally cause major incidents or outages. If the first parachute, high availability, is not sufficient or the incident is significant, disaster recovery can be employed to avoid any lengthy outage. The assumption is that the disaster-recovery plans in place can recover the required system in a timely manner. This is, of course, the guiding principle of disaster-recovery-plan authoring combined with an effective criticality assessment.

Once disaster recovery has been employed and the required systems have been recovered to a running state at the DR site, the business should assess the requirement to recover. IT services are usually not the first ones to be considered here, but once the decision has been made to recover, the return-to-normal (RTN) steps should be followed within the relevant plans. This is why disaster-recovery plans should include an RTN section.

First, having a disaster recovery plan removes the uncertainty of recovery and, second, any qualms because the disaster-recovery plans should have been tested.

Assumptions

While writing this book, I made some assumptions with regard to the level of experience you, as the reader, have. I assume you have general knowledge of the IT Infrastructure Library (ITIL); however, I am not going to test your knowledge of function names and processes. Though it helps, it is not essential to understand IT service-continuity management. If you are not familiar with ITIL, I would highly recommend reading about ITIL V3, as it is beneficial and can provide some good best practices. For the purpose of understanding IT service continuity and its management, it is not mandatory.

I also assume that you are familiar with some type of delivery process. Don't worry if you're fairly new to IT and have been tasked with IT service-continuity management, since a delivery process within a business delivers new IT systems and services.

About Me

I have worked in the IT industry for more than twenty-three years, starting in service desk/support and moving through systems-consultant and project-management roles to executive management. Having worked across multiple sectors, including both the public and private, my roles have been varied. Industries include health care, finance, construction, national government, road-user charging, engineering, oil and gas (both heavy oil and Liquefied Natural Gas (LNG) production). In these industries, one common theme had emerged: disaster recovery planning.

Today it is called IT service-continuity management.

IT Service-Continuity Management

IT service-continuity management is the process in which plans are put in place and managed to ensure that IT services can recover and continue should a serious incident occur. It's about not only reactive measures but also proactive measures—reducing the risk of a disaster in the first instance. More and more, ITSCM is focusing on proactive prevention measures such as testing and preparing for an event.

IT service continuity should apply a holistic approach to ensure IT services are healthy and can support the business. To determine which services are critical to a company's survival, we use a reliable tool to rate the services: the business-impact assessment (BIA), which touches on risk management. A risk assessment should identify the business risks from the systems and services.

The BIA is a document that clarifies a system's value to a business. To illustrate, a system in an organization will have a system owner, a business-based person who knows the importance of the system being assessed. The assessor is usually someone from the ITSCM or BCP part of the business. The assessor walks through the BIA, which comprises several questions concerning potential impact if the system were unavailable, or the regulatory impact if the system were unavailable. Ultimately, upon completing the document, a score is given, which determines the criticality of the system.

The outcome of the risk assessment and the BIA drives the IT service-continuity strategy. Organizations must adopt a balanced approach in which risk reduction and recovery are required in equal measure.

Likewise, an organization should attempt to reduce the single point of failure (SPOF) within its environment to reduce the risk of a major incident, which could cause major outages.

IT service continuity does draw one toward information technology, but even when looking at IT service-continuity planning, one must not be blinkered. Consider the external environment of other business departments and functions to determine whether they could impact, or even cause, an IT service-continuity event.

The concept of degraded service levels when IT service continuity is invoked is a strong one, and IT managers, CIOs, and business-continuity managers should remain firmly grounded. The trouble can start when senior management becomes aware of an IT service-continuity project and assumes all systems will be available. This magic (or, as I call it, the Disney experience) is a hard myth to break. IT service continuity is not cheap, but it does not have to cost the earth. Simply planning and testing your standard recovery methods thoroughly will enhance your organization's IT service-continuity maturity. How many of us carry out nightly, weekly, and even monthly backups only to never validate they have worked successfully?

One of the biggest hurdles faced by any project delivering IT service continuity is the absence of an established business-continuity planning (BCP) process. It's like asking for lottery numbers without first buying a lottery ticket. However odd this may appear, it happens a lot.

Then comes the real danger: the IT continuity-planning team could make the wrong assumptions, which could lead to expensive, ineffective recovery solutions. Likewise, if there is no BCP in place, the business may fail to highlight inexpensive recovery solutions and continue to purchase expensive and inefficient recovery solutions. More often than not, there is no BCP at all. IT services then attempts to retrofit or supply ITSCM for everything as no knowledge or BIA is pursued. The result is a costly and time-consuming exercise.

The perception that BCP is an IT responsibility is usually found in organizations with a low maturity level toward BCP and ITSCM. If an organization has an established BCP process, the frustration and challenge is then the alignment between ITSCM and BCP.

Business-continuity planning extends far beyond ITSCM. Other areas, depending on your organization's size, may include the following:

- Risk management
- Facilities management
- Supply-chain management
- Quality management
- Health and safety
- Knowledge management
- Emergency management
- Security
- Communications and marketing

The key to the BCP is to identify whom to call on if there is an event or disaster that will impact the business. For example, will we need someone in finance or someone in human resources (HR)? Once we identify the necessary business functions, we can focus on more detailed requirements, such as whether our identified resources require office space or transportation.

Once we have identified the who, when, and where of HR, we can then pinpoint what IT systems and services are required to support the HR function. Next, we enter the realm of ITSCM. Unfortunately, in some organizations, there is also a very real perception that disaster recovery is business-continuity planning. In some workplaces, I have seen IT recovery documents labeled as business-continuity planning. I will try not to belabor the point, but business-continuity planning is *not* IT service continuity. Yes, they dovetail, but both clearly have different roles to play in a major outage or disaster.

I like to differentiate between the two areas of IT service-continuity management: (1) the day-to-day management and upkeep is the **Delivery Stage**, and (2) the reacting to an incident or event is the **Execution Stage**. Thus, you are either in the management of IT service continuity's normal, daily DR plan review and testing, or else an event has occurred, and you must enter the **Execution Stage** to recover.

It sounds rather complicated and cumbersome, but, in short, we are making sure that the IT systems required to keep the business operating can support the business in its hour or two of need. How do we do this? It's actually quite simple.

Scope

Welcome to ITSCM 101!

It is worth mentioning that this book is not about project-management techniques or how to run projects; rather, it is designed to provide you with a clear understanding of what IT service continuity is, what is included in the scope of IT service continuity, and how to implement it without any distractions.

You will find that, besides my sense of humor, I have captured and consolidated the actions required into a process with the necessary supporting tools that can be used to provide effective IT service-continuity planning for your organization.

I have purposely omitted details regarding the generic project-management process and the wish-list items when discussing ITSCM or disaster recovery.

An organization's culture, structure, and strategic direction (both business and technology) can be key inputs in determining the scope of an effective ITSCM strategy.

Likewise, I have found that in some organizations where the ITSCM maturity level is lower than others, ITSCM has actually driven some areas of focus concerning technology utilization.

A great benefit can be derived from the involvement of people who have solid business and infrastructure knowledge. This, combined with their experience, can ensure that the basic fundamentals are considered when defining the scope of any such project.

First, ensure the scope of the project that is tasked to deliver IT service continuity focuses on the business's requirements and not the wish list of interested parties.

You will find out later that a project approach is a one-trick pony that usually produces minimal results as opposed to a process approach that delivers long-term benefits and results.

I have been involved in many ITSCM projects where the interested parties tried to use the project to get the latest and greatest technology, regardless of project or business needs. This is very prominent in IT service continuity, as usually, somewhere along the line, ITSCM requires some upgrades or enhancements to facilitate the required support.

One project I worked on required some disaster-recovery planning and then testing. A simple task, you might think. And it would have been—but for a senior stakeholder who, upon hearing of this project, immediately started advocating that the business had to pay $100,000 in licensing for the disaster-recovery project to continue. There was, of course, no requirement for this licensing. The senior stakeholder merely wanted to increase his license count, as he was overcommitted and did not want the CIO to be aware of his mistake.

The IT service-continuity or disaster-recovery scope should be simple, considering that only the required systems are targeted. Again, it is easy when engaging stakeholders to get drawn into thinking that all systems are essential to the business. In reality, only a handful will be.

In the UK, I worked in the transport industry with a government client. This private/public-sector company was dealing with the general public and keeping the motorway traffic flowing freely. A simple transaction was performed at a toll bridge, and then drivers were allowed to continue.

While I was wearing my IT service-continuity glasses, a simple IT service continuity solution should have been very easy to implement. However, when I engaged with the various business areas, it became apparent that they thought all of the system was critical. Why or how? Well, they were looking past the initial, immediate requirements. To provide effective ITSCM, the transaction had to be supported and then allowed to be processed to enable the public to continue on their journey. This should have been the end of the road (excuse the pun)—no more work required.

Needless to say, after some good workshops and risk-management-technique training, it was realized that only some parts were required. The project succeeded to provide a resilient and highly available system should any part of the system experience an event or outage.

So, when scoping an ITSCM project, there will be some assumptions.

Here are two major assumptions:

- Any disaster-recovery plan that is created will contain the procedures for restoring IT components, communications, services, and information following a disruptive event.

- "Information" refers to electronic information (e.g., data within databases and application files, and data on CDs, DVDs, or memory sticks).

It would be unfair and unjust to scope your ITSCM project based on many scenarios. Put another way, ITSCM is usually invoked when IT services are impacted. Non-IT events can also occur, causing major disruptions.

For example, an earthquake could render the data center unusable. This is one scenario of many, one that does not necessarily need to be considered. The real area of concern is the data center's unavailability, which could be due to an earthquake, flood, or building power failure. The key to effective ITSCM is to differentiate between the cause, the effect, and the impact.

Scoping an ITSCM project and taking these factors into consideration will streamline the speed of recovery.

Scope. Make sure it's clear, defined, and well known to avoid wasting time.

Why Do We Need IT Service Continuity?

Do we *really* need IT service continuity?

Picture this: You're in your car driving along the freeway, and an animal darts out in front of you. Do you really need brakes? Your immediate response might be yes, but you could live without them (not for long, I'll grant you). In fact, you could steer around the animal and then use the gears to slow down.

Let's consider a less dangerous scenario: You're in your car one morning, ready to go to work, but your car won't start. You can either walk to work (may not be feasible) or take a taxi, train, or bus. A late start means you have to stay late. Your boss might not be too impressed with your timekeeping, but you can survive in the short term. In fact, some may say we don't need the car at all.

Again, it boils down to the risk and cost–benefit argument. The question remains: Can your business survive without its IT systems for any length of time? More important, can it function?

It is an interesting question. A bank, for instance, would be in big trouble if it could not access its computer systems immediately. No cash means no customers, and no customers mean no business.

Another facet to IT systems availability is regulation. Many businesses that operate today are governed by regulatory standards and are normally accountable to governments. These regulatory requirements can often dictate that IT service continuity is in place to ensure the requirements placed on businesses are achievable.

This is true for the health sector as well. Yes, an operation can continue under the guidance of trained surgeons, but in today's world of technology where a patient's x-rays and blood results are electronic and available throughout the patient's hospital stay, this availability can pose many risks.

I worked in a hospital on various IT projects. One, in particular, was the refurbishment of the Accident and Emergency Department's frontline systems. It was a groundbreaking project that integrated radiology, pathology, and a new patient-booking system. Back in the day of no budgets, this project (deemed to be critical) was expected to be delivered no matter what; surgeons and doctors would access results within seconds of the data being uploaded and processed. However, only when the booking system failed did anyone realize that in its failing, the results were not available. How could this occur? Failure of dependencies being identified was deemed as the root cause. Consequently, all IT service-continuity planning that took place following this minor blip ensured that dependencies were identified early on.

The Impacts of Disaster Recovery

Disaster-recovery impacts are far, wide, and many, but a disaster is only a disaster if it's not planned for! So plan, plan, and plan again. As my granddad once said, "Measure things three times and cut only once." In other words, plan, test, plan, test, and plan again until you have total confidence that your systems will be available no matter what.

The impacts of disaster recovery are huge when recovery is executed with precision and care, thorough testing, and remediation, where required. All yield benefits when the real scenario hits.

Many companies back up their data but never restore it. I have been in workplaces where someone has asked for a deleted file to be recovered, only to find that it is corrupt and of no use. What happens if this is requested on a large scale once IT service continuity is invoked? Failure.

Imagine being the head of IT. An outage has just occurred, and the business-continuity plan has been invoked. You arrive at the alternative location to be met by the CEO, who is eerily calm. He knows his A-team is on the case and that everything is going to be OK, or so he thinks. He turns to you and asks, "How long before we are up and running again?" The worst-case scenario is that you have not reviewed—let alone tested—your IT recovery plan in six months, and you have no agreements in place to supply hardware to your new location.

In truth, many companies won't even have recovery plans to implement after a major incident. These companies will become a statistic because of their inability to produce goods or manufacture products. Customer retention is lost as competitors supply what they need to stay in business. Unfortunately, this is reality for a lot of companies. Even in today's world of natural disasters, terrorism, and technology outages, businesses continue to take unnecessary risks.

Let's remain positive, though. You *do* have plans (don't be a statistic!). You've tested them, and they are rock solid. With confidence you assure the CEO that your systems will be back up and running in hours. What a great feeling.

I worked in the police force for some time and experienced a disaster in which a new replacement radio system was rolled out, moving from analog to digital. However, upon rollout it was not tested in terms of disaster recovery to my grandfather's standard and, subsequently, left officers in need of assistance and unable to call for it. When I and some other officers went to check on them, we realized things were not under control, and the two first responders were actually being assaulted by six men. It is fortunate that we arrived before anyone was seriously injured.

The terrorist attacks of September 11 caused large-scale network outages. Some of the affected systems were the fiber-optic telecommunications services. Besides the financial impact to Wall Street firms from lost data connectivity, the loss of voice contact with friends and family greatly affected many individuals on that day.

I am not suggesting we can plan for every possibility; I am suggesting that we plan for some—the ones that we know could cause serious damage.

Measure three times and then cut once.

Trying to avoid the impacts of a disaster is a lottery, and time is better spent planning to recover from one. This scenario-based approach allows a stable, planned, and understood expectation of what will be achievable.

One must remember that it's not all negativity and black clouds. There are some companies that take the subject seriously enough to plan and test for most scenarios. Such companies gauge the impacts of disaster recovery and learn from them. Thus, they evolve into organizations that can stand the test of time and whatever life throws at them.

Disaster recovery can also improve the quality of human life; it may even save lives.

Types of Disaster Recovery

IT service continuity can be closely aligned with incident management; however, it is important to distinguish where it sits in terms of the ITIL framework. For those who are not familiar with the Information Technology Infrastructure Library (ITIL), it is a set of best practices for IT service management (ITSM) that focuses on aligning IT services with the needs of a business.

IT service continuity is positioned within the service design stage of the five stages of the service life-cycle model. ITSCM should be viewed holistically and considered throughout the design, construct, and operate phases of a system's life cycle.

In some circumstances, the actual design of a system may need to be amended to provide the required IT service-continuity requirements that are driven from the business.

Many types of disaster-recovery options are available to businesses today, ranging from the free to the very expensive. The popular ones include the following:

- Nothing at all—surprisingly, this is very common
- No disaster-recovery plan but good backup procedures
- A disaster-recovery plan but no resources in place
- A cold-site disaster-recovery plan

- A split-site disaster-recovery solution
- A hot-site disaster-recovery solution

Nothing at all

Nothing at all can be a popular choice. A simple system crash, equipment failure, or power surge is all it takes for a critical database to be wiped out. Unlike hardware or software, data are an even more valuable asset that cannot be replaced and should be protected. We all insure our cars, homes, and lives, don't we?

No disaster-recovery plan but good backup procedures

This option is the absolute minimum for any company, although how many actually backup and restore files to prove its working 100 percent correctly? If you work in an IT department and this is not happening, maybe now is the time to stand up and ask why.

A disaster-recovery plan but no resources in place

Once you have a level of maturity in your backup and archival procedures, ensure you have the resources to cope with an IT disaster. This extends beyond IT hardware availability to include hardware, software, employees, office space, remote-access capability, and communications between employees, such as mobile phones, vendor agreements, and support contracts that will aid in the recovery. This type of recovery can follow an ITSCM project that has begun compiling plans but then stops short.

A cold-site disaster-recovery plan

A quick and easy recovery option, a cold-site disaster-recovery plan is usually a reserved space in a data center in which to recover the systems. While it is a popular and cost-effective way for businesses to survive, the key is to ensure you have the resources to utilize it. This approach is commonly used when disaster recovery is outsourced. Resources include the technical expertise and skilled staff required to get those systems up and running securely to support the business.

A split-site disaster-recovery solution

A split-site disaster-recovery solution is a popular choice for businesses that have more than one location. Spreading the data center across two or more locations can be useful, depending on available infrastructure. Given today's virtualization and cloud-based services, this is more and more possible. The hybrid of this is Recovery as a Service (RaaS), where you buy your recovery services from a third party and they locate copies of your virtual servers in the cloud, ready to provision when necessary.

A hot-site disaster-recovery solution

The hot-site disaster-recovery solution is the premium option; it provides a second data center usually built to a lesser specification (in a disaster-recovery situation, the capacity required to run your business systems is less). The concept is to make available (within seconds) your critical and essential applications required to support the business, which requires the data used at the main data center to be replicated to the hot site. The second data center comes at a cost, along with the required maintenance to keep it up to date.

What can go wrong?

Disaster recovery is planning for the unexpected, which comes in many forms. Take, for example, an act of God or a higher being, human error, and, of course, run-of-the-mill infrastructure/facilities emergencies such as burst pipes and power failure.

I was fortunate (or unfortunate, depending on how you view it) to experience an IT disaster while working for a private company. The business had two data centers and, thankfully, I had not long implemented IT service continuity or carried out disaster-recovery planning. Having chosen the split-site solution, due to the business having many offices located throughout England and Wales, they were well prepared for what would follow. The main data center was located in what was thought to be a prime location—above ground level (no perceived water hazards and redundant power supplies with backup generators). One might say some level of high availability had been implemented.

The problem occurred during recent plumbing of the men's toilet twenty meters away. The plumber had inadvertently loosened a pipe that had been capped off above the data center some years ago. The result was a waterfall through the main data-center ceiling encompassing the racks of servers, storage, and network equipment.

Most amusing to see a data center being filled with water at an alarming rate, and even more amusing to watch the maintenance crew trying to find the shut-off valve, which took twenty minutes to locate as the one operative who knew the location was out of the office. Needless to say, lessons were learned, the first being, *ensure key operational staff is aware of the water shut-off valves and switches*.

Four hours later, service was resumed. IT services were restored within minutes, but the physical hazard reduction took longer, which meant office workers had to wait to safely return to the office.

This incident highlights the direct correlation between the business-continuity planning team and the IT service-continuity team.

It's no good having a data center if you don't have any people to use the systems housed within it.

Traditional Recovery Methods

At one time, systems and services were provided on physical hardware. Prior to that, pen and paper were used. Or, if you fall into the more mature age bracket, you would have used chalk and slate boards. In the days of pen and paper, the recovery plan entailed making a copy using the photocopier and filing it away. If the original was lost, much time was spent looking for that copy.

Nowadays, convenience has misled people into believing that recovery is easier, or maybe instantaneous and more effortless.

Although computers have made life easier, technology is developing at such an alarming rate that the complexity of the systems that require recoverability has also increased. The result is a ripple effect. When recovering these systems, more time and technology is required. The number of resources increases with the complexity of the systems being recovered.

Ten years ago, storage would have been fairly basic—disks in an array with some redundancy. Today, storage is a solid state with write error checking algorithms, combined with virtualization.

The traditional approach to recovery was tape based, and this effective medium of recovery was just that simplistic. The tape schedule provided a structured methodology of what tapes were required and when they could be reused. When trying to recover entire servers, however, this data-recovery process became complicated. It was quicker to simply rebuild from scratch in most cases.

In the eighties, the systems were basic and backed up to tape. To recover, the backup tape would be located, and then the restore would commence. One or two operations were required to get you back to where you were following an outage or major incident. Obviously, restoring from tape takes longer than restoring from disk—hence the reason to move away from tape for backups and to utilize them only for archiving. Now, disk to disk is preferred; alternatively, optical archival systems are utilized.

Today's systems are more complex. A typical system will exist on a server (a piece of tin) and will have some sort of connection. It might be a database, a web server, or another system. Such complexity means higher costs due to the extra resources required to recover the systems, along with the additional hardware. Though advances in virtualization have reduced the complexity, where this technology is not in use, recovery costs are increased.

Company X would either purchase an off-the-shelf software product and install it on their hardware or get a provider to supply the chosen product on hardware and support it via a maintenance contract. Either way, IT service continuity was seldom used and understood even less.

Faced with a problem, you would struggle to quickly restore your systems or services. This model was high risk but culturally accepted.

Today, if the risk is high, then a spare piece of hardware is procured and located a practical distance from the primary host. In the event of a disaster, the IT service could be up and running fairly quickly, depending on what means the users had to access the secondary host.

Gone are the days of just utilizing a disaster-recovery (DR) plan. The new technological world has enabled a tiered approach to enable systems to fail over and recover scenarios. Traditional recovery approaches would entail executing DR when a significant incident occurs, which might include major component failure, depending on the build of the physical hardware. Move over, DR; high availability (HA) has just entered the building.

It is important to reiterate, however, that high availability is not disaster recovery.

High availability supports the potential for component failure, which, today, provides more convenience when executing your disaster-recovery plans.

Current Recovery Methods

Today, virtualization has taken hold, and vast numbers of organizations are moving toward this new nirvana. Virtualization yields many benefits, like the speed in which virtual servers can be recovered. What's more, virtual-server infrastructure is cost effective and quick to provision. The benefits roll in when a business really harnesses the power of virtualization and the cloud.

The cloud provides a highly resilient and available location for hosting the servers required for the essential systems of today's enterprise. Thus, Recovery as a Service (RaaS)—an innovative use of the cloud—provides the corporate body with an area where its critical systems can be recovered quickly and effortlessly. As a service, the corporate body does nothing but pay the invoice and know that its services will be available should there be an outage.

Gartner is an American information technology research and advisory firm providing technology related insight. They predict that by 2017, 35 percent of midsize businesses will adopt cloud-based recovery services. Despite this prediction, many organizations rely on their own trusted recovery methods. As technology has improved, so has the recovery capability.

This is more prevalent in the storage world today, where storage arrays have next to zero recovery time frames using a synchronous technology to ensure data are written to two locations at once. The two locations could be separated, with many miles between data centers.

Virtualization is not always possible due to a number of factors. Legacy systems plague IT managers, for they have hardware dependencies and may well use dongles for licensing. Then there is the software that clearly defines within its license agreement that it cannot be virtualized. These systems face the biggest challenges in relation to ITSCM. Costs skyrocket when dealing with physical hardware-based systems, including increased support costs, for these legacy systems also inhibit the potential to virtualize.

Virtualization is not a silver bullet. Yes, it aids deployment of new servers and can provide some level of high availability while reducing operating costs. But the physical world is not without its tricks. Some products in the marketplace will back up the physical server as a recoverable image file on a network location, making recovery as simple as switching on the replacement hardware and loading the image of the failed server.

How do you know it is time?

So, how do you know it's time to execute IT service continuity? When someone is screaming at you that something has happened, that the photocopier is not working anymore, or that the big red light on the wall is flashing?

Deciding whether or not to execute IT service continuity normally sits very high up on the food chain, someone at the CIO level or higher. This responsibility can be delegated, however. Most subordinates would not execute it unless authorized to do so. Why? Usually in a live situation in which a business has executed its IT service-continuity plans, the business will be running at less-than-optimal efficiency. Also, the recovery sites are normally geared to provide a reduced capacity in terms of performance; thus, day-to-day operations are affected.

The rationale for deciding is derived from corporate risk tables and the potential impact of systems or service loss on the business. Many large organizations will have a business-continuity manager or a crisis team to assist in the decision to invoke process and also to aid coordination efforts for a response.

Once the recovery-time objective (RTO) for a system or service has been defined, the IT service-continuity manager, assisted by the IT operational teams, can decide which disaster-recovery technologies are best suited to the situation. For example, if the RTO for Application X is one hour, redundant data backup on external hard drives could be the best solution. If the RTO is seven days, then tape, compact disk, or off-site disk storage may be more cost effective. However, a near-zero RTO (for a time-sensitive operation, like a bank) may require a more modern "mirrored" technology. Likewise, the definition of the recovery-point objective, or point in time at which work must be restored following an event, can drive the technology and implementation choice.

More mature ITSCM organizations will take a service-oriented approach to continuity. That is, they will utilize several different technologies with ITSCM. When a new system is in project delivery, a suitable technology would be chosen to match the RTO and RPO. This menu selection simplifies the options available to the project-delivery teams and removes the ambiguity associated with disaster-recovery plan creation.

Many businesses will be happy to make do with a close-of-business RPO; they are happy restoring data, systems, and activities to the prior day's close of business in the event of a disaster or incident. Others (e.g., a bank) will have a point-of-failure RPO; in other words, the data, systems, services, and activities must be recovered to the point that they failed.

The BIA will tease out key areas where a loss of service would impact the business in various ways.

Key areas can include, but are not limited to, the following:

- Lost productivity
- Damaged reputation
- Revenue impact
- Financial performance

Narrow down to the employees and equipment impacted by the number of hours lost. With respect to damaged reputation, this can extend to customers, suppliers, and associated financial markets and, in turn, can negatively impact revenue. Consider, for example, direct costs incurred and potential compensatory payments, which would cause lost future revenue and potential investment losses.

The BIA does not only look at the impact to the business. Some companies combine the BIA with their criticality assessments. What's the difference? The criticality assessment—also known as the criticality information assessment (CIA)—provides another view of the system or service and typically measures the confidentiality level. For example, does the system utilize public information or company information? Does the data that the system uses require any special regulatory requirements (for systems that handle financial data or are subject to financial reporting conditions in terms of the integrity level of the data)? The CIA may also highlight the availability requirements the business needs to ensure that their process remains stable in times of need.

So that the approach is pragmatic and achievable, it is helpful if the BIA is conducted by those familiar with

IT service continuity. Note that the BIA should be conducted using a top-down approach. In other words, focus on identifying the critical business processes to aid the systems that support those critical processes.

The dovetailing of ITSCM and BCP is critical, and good relationships must exist between disaster-recovery and business-continuity planning. Often these can be fragmented, leaving unprotected areas or risks.

Sometimes the BIA and the assessments process can be carried out by someone who has no concept of the context in which he or she is conducting the assessment. As such, the interviewer is led by the interviewee, resulting in the system or service being classified as critical and the RTO being near zero, which, while achievable, is expensive. Often, BIAs reveal dependencies on other resources that can be a single point of failure.

Areas of Concern

During ITSCM, many issues may arise, as different stakeholders have different priorities. If you adopt the process approach, the following issues will dissolve as process and structure remove any uncertainty:

Expectations versus Reality

Expectations versus reality can be problematic when it comes to IT service continuity because most businesspeople do not fully understand IT services and the infrastructure required to provide them. Thus, a domestic view is adopted, since most people have computers or tablets at home with high-speed Internet and experience very little outage. Such service is then expected in the workplace, where the environment is more complex and usually involves dependencies of multiple systems, compounded by the complex security requirements mandated by security-conscious companies.

Quality of External Service Providers

The quality of external service providers is important when a disaster-recovery scenario is playing out. You hope for top-quality providers under contract to get your business back up and running as defined in your service-level agreement.

Quality of Service-Level Agreements

Thoroughly reviewing a commercial-services agreement to ensure that it addresses the major issues from a business standpoint can be a challenge. Does the contract support the statement of work in terms of quality and availability of your systems? Do its basic metrics and levels of support provide your required recovery time frames? These sound like basic key points, but I have often found a critical system to be needed in two hours when in fact the SLA states a longer recovery time.

Management and Renewal of Agreements

I cannot tell you the number of times I have asked corporate licencing departments about a licence status, only to learn that it expired several months ago and that it's being renegotiated. I am not sure if this is a stalling technique from the finance department or if it's a genuine status; either way, make sure you're covered.

Another time, failure of equipment at a client site meant a call to Cisco, only to find out the maintenance had expired on the device. They were adamant they could not help until the maintenance was purchased.

System Ownership ("New" Management Team)

This is a classic. New management comes in, unaware of an existing plan (if any plan exists). Then disaster strikes, and *boom!*— new management fails to respond or attempts an unplanned response, usually resulting in more damage or a failed response. The key, then, is to ensure ITSCM responsibilities are assigned to a role rather than a person. In addition, ITSCM awareness sessions should take place with senior stakeholders and ITSCM managers quarterly.

Security of Software Media and Documentation

Security and media location should go hand in hand. Who can honestly say, yes, I know where my media are for my critical systems? Not many, I would think, if you're being honest.

Some organizations have agreements with storage and archival providers who can resolve this issue.

The answer in ITIL language is the Definitive Media Library (DML), a secure information-technology repository that, when combined with the configuration database, provides an effective release management tool. The

CMDB is the DNA of the data center and company alike.

With the explosion of cloud-based services and the uncertainty of data sovereignty increasing, the location of company data has become a key issue. Security and governance oversee the bigger data concerns relating to cloud-based services, but it is just as important within IT service continuity to ensure critical data and media are secure yet accessible. Recovery success can depend on access to media and data during an incident or disaster.

More recent products provide electronic storage facilities for your media. Electronic DMLs provide easy, readily available access combined with the required security.

Note that if these DMLs are hosted locally, they themselves should be covered within your ITSCM strategy, as losing this system is akin to losing the key to the key box.

Process

Understanding the process is crucial in successful IT service continuity. No matter the size of your company, if you take a process approach to ITSCM, delivery will be one thing: consistent.

During a personnel change or senior-management rotation, a quality manager or leader will scrutinize ITSCM, as it is a high-risk area. Despite their good intentions, these quality managers typically respond by going into solution mode, which is to try and fix it—once. As a result, the project starts to remediate and plans are redrafted. The testing that is performed can sometimes be successful; sometimes it becomes a tick-box exercise, and when it is completed, the project closes down. Some leaders will not only remediate but replicate their success.

They have tested, failed, remediated, and tested successfully, not only in invoking a DR process or service but also achieving ITSCM success. Moving forward, they can sleep easy knowing that their business will be recoverable.

The project-versus-process approach is a hot topic in ITSCM. I am not condoning ITSCM or DR projects but merely stressing that a process approach will yield a better return on investment than a project approach. I have led many projects using the process approach, blending the project with the process until eventually the organization has a mature and repeatable ITSCM capability.

The following overview of the ITSCM process can be applied to all businesses. Keep in mind that this is the management of IT service continuity, and not IT service-continuity execution, a subtle nuance that focuses on managing instead of actively delivering continuity once invoked.

Although ITIL is the most widely accepted approach to IT service management, it does so at a high level; thus, the detailed process is somewhat lacking in explanation, specifically in relation to IT service-continuity management.

ITIL provides a clear, cohesive set of best practices drawn from the public and private sectors internationally; there are good explanations and examples of how to apply it. The ITSCM process, on the other hand, has suffered; this is the reason that I have written this book. ITSCM, in my experience, is one of the most valued and one I feel passionately about.

The details of ITSCM (and the environment that impacts it) are vague. How can one thoroughly understand ITSCM from fifty thousand feet? My goal is to bring you down to the ten-foot view so that you have an effective and reliable reference to apply ITSCM.

The ITSCM process covers training, testing, and design and starts with a new system or a new service, or from a change to an existing system or service. An alternative initiation may be from a portfolio review, which the business may carry out as part of an application portfolio management (APM) exercise. APM drives efficiency by design.

Application rationalization is implemented, thereby reducing capital costs and ongoing support costs by removing redundancy in the applications that are deployed within an organization. It is common in large organizations; they may well have more than one application doing the same or a similar job, which can be combined into one.

Either way, once initiated, the first cab off the rank is the criticality of all the systems or services that support the business, which is then reviewed or assessed depending on the ITSCM maturity level within your business.

The below diagram shows the ITSCM process at a high level.

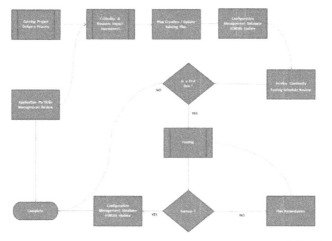

While the criticality assessment can be done in a number of ways, it normally takes the format of a business-impact assessment (BIA). This initial task is paramount in ascertaining the importance of a system to your organization.

Without this first step, you might be wasting a lot of time, energy, and money on systems or services the business does not require if there were a significant outage or disruption.

The initial change of a system or a new system process would normally be done by either your own internal delivery process for projects or by a supplier. Either way, the project could be delivered by using a traditional methodology, such as the Office of Government Commerce (OGC) PRINCE2, or an Agile methodology such as DSDM.

47

There are ITSCM considerations when a new system is being delivered or requested, such as system architecture and system design, components of ITSCM. The system design may change, depending on the criticality and the ITSCM requirement of the system.

How would ITSCM impact the design of a system?

Let's take, for example, a simple e-mail system rollout; a simple, traditional rollout may be a mail server on each site. Following a BIA, you find that the system is actually critical, so the business will require a recovery-time objective (RTO), which is the acceptable amount of time to restore the function, such as one hour.

Can your IT teams rebuild the e-mail system in an hour? Are the network links between sites supported to that level of availability? Chances are, this service cannot be recovered within an hour.

Thus, initially the e-mail system could be restructured in terms of architecture design based on the IT service continuity required from the solution to support the business.

IT service-continuity engagement must occur early on in your IT systems project delivery. Also, as highlighted via the network links, ensure that any suppliers of such dependencies can meet the required availability.

Next is a subprocess that resonates throughout the whole of ITSCM—the criticality definition—and calls out the key status of your application in terms of risk and the business's level of dependency on it.

A business-impact assessment (BIA) differentiates critical (urgent) and noncritical (nonurgent) organization systems or services. For critical systems or services, disruption is regarded as unacceptable. Perceptions of acceptability are affected by the cost of recovery solutions. A function may also be considered critical if dictated by law or regulation.

For each critical (in scope) system or service, two values are then assigned:

- **Recovery-Point Objective (RPO)**—the acceptable latency of data that will not be recovered

- **Recovery-Time Objective (RTO)**—the acceptable amount of time to restore the system

RPO is the acceptable amount of data loss that is unrecoverable following an outage. Alternatively the amount of time once a system has been recovered of acceptable data loss. (e.g., a 30 minute RPO, allows for 30 minutes of data loss after recovering the system).

RTO, however, is the time in which the business will recover the system (e.g., the system may have a two-hour RTO, which means the system will be recovered and up and running within two hours from the outage).

The world of ITSCM uses these two metrics frequently, but other factors should be considered when looking at system recovery. To increase ITSCM capability, we must look past the metrics of RTO and RPO to meet service-level agreements as set out by a BIA.

The two other metrics to consider are as follows:

- **Recovery Consistency Characteristics (RCC)**—data integrity within the business systems and processes

- **Recovery Object Granularity (ROG)**—level of objects that can be recovered within a system or process

RTO and RPO, without considering recovery consistency characteristics (RCC), can be risky; thus, any ITSCM work should look at the RCC also.

RCC considerations, in addition to RTO and RPO in the business-impact analysis, focus on the integrity of business data and processes in complex application environments such as an ERP system.

Targets for RCC normally increase with the criticality of the underlying business data.

So, a logistics and banking-related business process may have a higher RCC requirement than that of a customer relationship management system or a human resources system.

RTO combined with RPO and RCC is a good practice; however, we should also consider the recovery object granularity (ROG), which is the level of objects that a recovery solution is capable of recovering (i.e., a storage volume or disk, a database subset, or a particular area).

Often RTO and RPO are seen as the initial one-stop shop for ITSCM and disaster-recovery coverage, but other metrics help to ensure an appropriate recovery capability is present and available.

Harvested by the business-impact assessment, the recovery requirements are then used to plan for potential threats and risks. These can include but are not limited to

- earthquakes;
- floods;
- terrorism;
- thefts; and
- cyber attacks.

Once the recovery requirements are identified, the planning can commence based on these identified scenarios. In respect to scenario-based planning, this methodology is effective and realistic; the only downside is the many permutations of the threats and risks. In this case, a threat modeling technique can enhance the outcome.

Once used only by insurance companies, these tools are now more widely understood and used to enhance businesses' response in readiness for an outage or incident.

Threat modeling usually starts at the site level, where the initial site characteristics are acknowledged and the analysis parameters are defined. One might take into account the type of earthquakes or hurricanes that occur in the region, the intensity of past tremors, and the potential wind speeds particular to a region. Once these parameters have been defined, we can then better predict the potential damage and model that level of damage.

Other factors to consider concern the site facility. For example, when was the facility constructed? What type of construction is it (steel or concrete)? Is it cyclone proof? Answering such questions will help you plan an effective response. High-level threat modeling is as detailed as ITSCM gets; business-continuity management should be comprehensive and should provide the modeled data for consideration when planning ITSCM.

Clearly, ITSCM is IT focused, and some may argue that this information is irrelevant. I am simply advocating that being informed is key to the process.

It's easy to assume that events to be modeled for are events that affect the site and its facilities. Pandemics and terrorism are other areas of concern. While it is true that pandemic modeling usually lends itself more to business with respect to staff absenteeism and productivity, it is useful to highlight the IT services required for staff to work from home if they were required to do so.

When discussing ITSCM, the topic of terrorism brings to mind the numerous attacks that have affected many lives and businesses. Terrorism is normally covered in the scenario where the site is unavailable, or where there is a wider disruption to business. As such the response would be detailed and thoroughly tested.

Configuration Management

Everything has its place.

Asset tracking is essential to reduce costs and maintain an efficient department; thus, most large corporate businesses employ a configuration management database (CMDB).

What is a CMDB?

A configuration management database (CMDB) is a repository that acts as a data warehouse for information-technology (IT) organizations and departments. It holds a collection of IT assets commonly referred to as configuration items (CIs), as well as the descriptive relationships between such assets.

For example, a company may have System X, which consists of two servers and one workstation. The CMDB would hold a record for each of the servers and also a record for the workstation. These records would break down into the operating system versions, if present, and the software installed on each device. Such attributes are then collated. The mapping between objects provides a clearer picture to help aid support.

When populated, the repository becomes a means of understanding how critical business assets, such as information systems, are composed, what their upstream sources or dependencies are, and what their downstream targets are. The term CMDB is a general term, but many vendors offer this capability. Some form their central purpose around applications and software and can sometimes relate to the application portfolio management processes. While a more traditional CMDB is related to hardware and their relationships, this covers the software aspect as well.

Configuration items (CIs) include not just computers, servers, monitors, and networking equipment. It is easy to forget documentation either in the written or electronic form. Such documents are the glue of some organizations, and yet because paper is recognized as last-decade technology, it can be forgotten in areas that are business critical.

How many organizations have business-continuity plans neatly packaged in binders atop the executive's shelf, complete with version control—yet in the event of a disaster would be left on that shelf? Many, I can assure you. How difficult would it be to keep an electronic copy of that binder and reference it in the configuration management database, along with its relationship to the IT service-continuity management plan and respective supporting documents?

When IT service-continuity plans are created, they too must be recorded within the CMDB. That way, you'll have an audit of the recovery plans being created and maintained. If the CMDB is utilized correctly, you'll have a repository of your recovery plans and a schedule for ongoing testing and maintenance.

Once the CMDB has been updated, the business can conduct a monthly service-continuity review by interrogating the CMDB. Then, you'll know if a system is due for testing and, more importantly, the last test date and result. The selected system or service can then be tested. If the CMDB is accurate and up to date, then reporting on what is outdated and what needs updating becomes a lot easier.

On a side note, the subprocess of testing is twofold. A desktop walk-through occurs during year one and a full-system-recovery test during year two. This approach keeps the recovery requirements up to date in terms of testing procedure, and the expected reactions can be confirmed on paper without the unnecessary resources used during full-system testing.

Recap

Following is a recap of the ITSCM overview:

Initial Steps

Document a disaster-recovery strategy if you are starting at the beginning or are an IT professional who has extra time. That is, ensure key business processes are clearly understood and supported. (In reality, you grab a coffee and move on to the next activity, evaluation.) Note that we are talking about evaluation of the applications and their current DR-plan status. Try not to go straight into solution mode.

Evaluation

Review the current system ITSCM capabilities, if any exist. Chances are, there will be none, and when you talk to technical people, they will by habit immediately go into solution mode and start suggesting that this SQL database be replicated to somewhere else, and that a particular data set be copied to Location Y.

STOP! Evaluate and clearly document what is what, and where. Avoid technical-level conversations until later. Determine structure and ownership of major business processes, which is paramount, as it will help build your stakeholder lists for planning purposes. Determine the IT systems that support the identified business processes.

Determine current user expectations and IT capabilities.

Assessment

Here we focus on learning and information for learning and improving (an interactive process). Look at the required systems and services, and assess if any recovery methods that do exist would work if implemented immediately—as in right now! You may find that some systems have outdated solutions or need a quick tweak. Remember, this is a quick visual assessment, as a full review will be performed later.

Risk Management

To risk or not to risk. That is the question.

OK, so risk management does exist, and it is very real. In fact, there are standards associated with the whole topic of risk management. Here we are talking about the corporate risk-management approach within your organization. Typically, companies (normally larger ones) will have a corporate risk or assurance team that visits early on to gauge how the systems or services should be assessed and classified to ensure they meet the required availability that your plans will provide.

Really, do we need to analyze and reanalyze? No, let's keep the process simple. Protect what is dear to you, but always make sure the business wants protection.

The inherent risks associated with ITSCM can include the following:

- The failure of the business to embrace ITSCM process and procedures. Many ITSCM projects do not get completed; people come in and "play" with ITSCM and then get bored and move on. I have seen this time and again within organizations.

- Budget availability. Businesses sometimes want something for nothing and expect you to deliver full ITSCM across all their perceived critical and essential applications—all for twenty dollars.

- ITSCM processes focus on the technical, not on what the business needs. Refer to my point earlier about avoiding technical conversations early on; it is a downward spiral. You'll be left with few ITSCM plans that can provide the recovery-time objectives that the business requires.

Planning

At the heart of ITSCM is planning, the most important stage of the process.

The system's priority layer (this is what needs to be protected) is the first step in the planning stage. Here we name what we are going to protect.

In an ideal world, the way your organization usually delivers projects will include ITSCM as standard; thus, it will no longer be omitted. Operations may have been given a project via delivery teams; only to ask what ITSCM planning has been done. "Nothing" is the answer (*oh, sorry, we didn't realize we had to do that!*). Or, ITSCM is not fully understood, so project-delivery teams toss it into the too-hard basket and do nothing (*but infrastructure does backups, so we are OK!*).

There are many ways to plan for an event that would impact our business as usual, but it is here we ensure we cover the basic scenarios.

Scenario-based planning is key to achieve success; in fact, planning covers the following areas:

- Risk assessment
- Prevention
- Preparedness
- Response
- Recovery

To plan is to be prepared; to not plan is to fail!

When analyzing your readiness, consider the following factors:

- Determine if there are any regulatory, environmental, cultural, or contractual constraints

- Ensure that the IT service-continuity plan aligns with the business-continuity plan and is documented

- Reduce any gaps between the business-continuity plan and what the IT service-continuity plan can recover; document these and create a remediation plan

Scenarios to include are

- fire;
- flood;
- terrorism;
- data-centre unavailability/power failure; and
- physical access denied.

Scenario-based planning is key to successful recovery, allowing a realistic response to be planned and resourced effectively.

It will not be 100 percent accurate but will provide enough detail to ensure the recovery process flows and details are covered. Who, for example, will perform the recovery actions? When will these actions be performed? What systems will be affected, and how will this work be done?—the who, when, what, and how.

When looking at plan creation in line with the process diagram shown earlier, it is good practice to standardize the format of all the plans created. Create a template to be used as your master template.

Ideally, each site or business unit will have a site IT disaster-recovery plan documenting IT system-recovery responsibilities, procedures, and the return-to-normal (RTN) instructions.

These master templates should be prepared for all levels of the ITSCM, including the

- **System Recovery Plan**—for each individual system to be recovered, and the
- **Site Recovery Plan**—for each site that is to be recovered.

As indicated previously, these should be treated as controlled documents; therefore, it is important to include on the front the name of the recovery plan, the version of the document, and other pertinent information, such as system owner, RPO, RTO, criticality rating, plan custodian, and possibly a business support representative.

A clear, formal document structure is best, including key areas of discussion for the recovery-plan reader.

The recovery plan should be written in a language an eleven-year-old could read and understand. The eleven-year-old does not necessarily have to be a subject-matter expert in the system or service; the recovery plan should be able to be followed by a non-system expert since the procedural steps to recover the system or service would be done by an industry professional.

Other key pieces of information to capture include the following:

- IT system owner
- IT system custodian
- IT site coordinator
- Revisions of the document with comments
- Document distribution list
- System-recovery accountability (both lead and deputy roles)
- Background information and summary, including a small, brief architecture map/diagram
- Scope of the recovery plan
- Recovery prerequisites
- Recovery instructions
- Return-to-normal (RTN) instructions
- Contacts list

The background information and summary should detail a high-level diagram showing the system and dependencies. Other useful items are the number of system users, software, hardware, server infrastructure, client infrastructure (useful for non-web-based applications), and system vendors.

The scope should include a general and quick overview of the procedures and steps necessary in the event of a disaster. It should also mention the systems that are covered by the plan and specify what will be recovered.

The recovery prerequisites should define what is required for a successful recovery. For example, a system's prerequisites may be available networking, networking switch equipment, infrastructure services (such as Dynamic Host Configuration Protocol [DHCP]), or directory services (such as Microsoft Active Directory). All should be documented and referenced where applicable. Thus, if the directory services are a prerequisite, then these should be referenced in the recovery plan for this service and any other related services.

The recovery instructions—the steps to recover the system or service—are explained at the operational-instruction level but can reference procedures. A best practice is to keep the required procedure-level instructions available within the recovery plan to ensure the recovery team is working with what is required. This also clarifies what should be done, by whom, and when.

The return-to-normal (RTN) instructions detail how to return the system or service to its normal operating environment or state. Do not confuse this with the steps to recover. The analogy I like to use involves the car. The car, for instance, is fine and in working order. The recovery plan may be to ride a bike if the car fails. The RTN instructions explain how to repair the car and make sure it is working as it was.

Recovery plans should include client recovery as well as systems or service recovery. Many applications are not web enabled and require a client to be installed on the user's computer. This client software should also be recoverable, and the user-recovery plan should account for this. It is fair to assume that the client-recovery plan is a subset of the system/service-recovery plan. This should be tested independently to ensure the recovery steps are detailed sufficiently to permit successful recovery.

Once the plan is structured and the relevant details are captured, including the client-recovery aspect (if required), the next step is to confirm license capacity. This is an opportunity to sanity check the license requirements and confirm that the recovery procedures include this aspect.

You may think this is odd. I mention it because, during testing of one particular system, the recovery failed due to a license-file requirement. But one could only get a new license by e-mailing a request to an e-mail address that—surprise, surprise—was not monitored outside business hours. That is, the RPO and RTO were not met, and the system recovery was delayed considerably.

Testing

Make sure it does what you think it will.

Knowing that you're going to break a major system and then recover it is immensely satisfying. This is the fun bit! You are being allowed to break something that people really rely on and regard as special. While it sounds rather weird, that roller coaster of emotions—once agreement is provided to take a system or service down—is something you should savor but be prepared for.

Removing an ERP system is like cutting the flow of blood to the brain for most businesses. Initially, panic sets in, but having confidence in the good planning beforehand quickly reassures you that service will be restored. Obviously, poor planning means things can go wrong. You can go from hero to zero in ten seconds flat, so always check your plans and test regularly.

Various types of testing are available, but the key ones to consider in relation to ITSCM are the following:

- Standalone testing
- Integrated testing
- Site testing

If you're lucky, you are part of an organization that is aware of how useful testing can be; it makes life much easier. Imagine an organization that views your testing as a waste of time.

Time is money when a business cannot operate.

Standalone

Standalone testing assures you the system on its own will function and should be the precursor to any integrated testing. This can be quick and, when there are a lot of dependencies, can cause errors when these integration dependencies are missing. The trick here is to document the behavior of standalone and then keep these available for integration testing to assist in identifying when dependent systems are not available. This double-jeopardy approach covers all angles and will take more time, but you will reap the rewards later on. Standalone testing can be misleading when the dependencies are all available, and a test indicates that all recovery steps work without error. In standalone testing, ensure that dependencies are clearly defined and examined.

Integrated

Integrated testing provides a holistic view of system recovery. In reality, though, recovering all of your systems in a scenario is somewhat extreme. As I mentioned earlier, systems or services within a corporate environment should be identified and classified in line with the corporate risk tables within that organization. This will draw out the systems or services that are required to have IT service-continuity plans in place. The level of system or services required will not usually include all systems. As such, that invisible line is where the integration is broken. One should perform integration testing of the required core systems to ensure they will still function as expected.

Site

Site testing is the full monty; if you are carrying out site testing, your maturity level in IT service-continuity management is high. Site testing provides a thorough understanding of which systems are reliant upon others, and the dependency is mapped and understood.

Due to the impact on the business, site testing is rare and is normally performed biannually, depending on the industry sector. Banking and other sectors that are heavily regulated may perform site testing more frequently.

Remediation

Very rarely does anything go right the first time.

So you have completed your standalone testing, and something did not go as planned. Well, that is normal. In fact, I remember carrying out some initial testing at a client site, only to hear that when it had failed (which was expected), the client was ecstatic. The CIO knew then that it could be identified and fixed.

You may encounter negative people when you test and fail. Be prepared for criticism, and move on.

It is a great approach from management, but after some time, the novelty does wear off. Remediation is reviewing what went wrong and updating your plan so that when you retest, it runs smoothly and completes as expected. To ensure this happens, meet with the testing team and walk through each task until you pinpoint where it failed.

Here you open the floor to suggestions. At this technical level, someone (usually technically minded) will suggest a work-around. Update the plan accordingly and retest.

Retesting

Retesting is for those who want to do it right.

This is not the retesting that comes later, such as the following year. Nor is it a scheduled test. Retesting follows the remediation work that was required due to the plan failing upon first activation.

Allow me to elaborate.

You create a plan. It looks good. You discuss testing the plan, covering every step required with the subject-matter experts, system administrators or operational teams that will actually perform the specific recovery actions.

Then you can start your testing. It is the first test, the one that, in an ideal world, will work flawlessly and without any interruptions.

Now it's time for retesting. Your first test failed, but this can be a good thing, remember (the glass is half full). You and your team remediate the plan. Upon retesting, you should have no issues. I suggest using this phase as an iterative process in which you are dealing with a very complicated system and wish to gently build confidence within your recovery team and plan.

Schedule

What goes on the schedule?

I noticed one IT service-continuity manager had a particularly unique method of filing his plan-remediation activities and schedule. The business asked me to assist with ITSCM, and after my second day, I asked this manager where I could find the schedule of testing. He replied, "It's up there." Sure enough, on his wall was a line of yellow Post-it Notes.

At a minimum, the schedule's content should include the following:

- Name of system or service
- Last test date
- Last test result
- Last test type
- Next test date

The minimum can be expanded to include these areas:

- Recovery metrics such as RPO and RTO
- Remediation required
- Comments
- System owner and system contact information

Who manages the schedule?

The IT service-continuity manager or business-continuity manager manages the schedule. It will likely fall to operational management to ensure IT service continuity is in place and working. It's not unusual for the business-continuity manager to also manage it and provide governance throughout the testing process. Alternatively, the security team may oversee this function.

Either way, the results should be recorded and published to the business representative or to the wider business community.

Resources, Roles, and Responsibilities

Given IT service continuity's focus on planning around disasters, make sure the plan identifies who will react in a scenario. When writing recovery plans, refer to people's roles instead of their names to keep documents current. Roles can be quickly referenced in the corporate organizational chart, rather than names, which change as people leave the organization.

While focusing on roles and responsibilities, it is good practice to ensure that each site or business unit has a nominated IT-DR site coordinator who

- declares or coordinates when a disaster has occurred;
- leads execution of the IT site recovery plan; and
- contributes to the currency of the IT site recovery plan.

The emergency-response team (ERT) is a group of assigned individuals familiar with their responsibilities should IT service continuity be invoked. The ERT should meet at least once a quarter to review the various elements associated with its role. These elements can be combined into one document and stored securely online or in a safe at the assembly location. Document revision should be utilized as well to ensure the last revision date is maintained. In addition, conduct regular reviews so that the content remains up to date and accurate.

At a minimum, you should include the following:

- ERT response plan
- Communication plan
- ERT resource plan

ERT Response Plan

The ERT response plan documents team members and their respective contact numbers in an emergency. It also details the team's assembly location (if required) and the agreements that support the assembly location, such as the shared-tenancy agreement, number of desks, hardware to make available, and communication methods. It should also detail Internet connectivity so that the ERT is fully mobilized and available globally, if required.

Communication Plan

The communication plan should detail the methods of communication between the ERT and management for decision-making purposes. This may seem trivial, but ERT comprises people from different parts of the business. In a normal operating environment, decision makers and lines of reporting are clear. In a crisis, however, when the ERT is operational, direction is less clear. With the stress and pressure of responding to a crisis, confusion ensues or, worse, a breakdown in communication.

ERT Resource Plan

The resource plan details the resources, including the ERT members, and specifies the following:

- Team members and roles
- Assembly location
- Assembly location supporting documents (shared-tenancy agreement)
- Hardware and software available at the assembly location
- Alternative data-center location (if required) for systems/service restoration
- Communication devices and their location (agreements supporting this, if required, such as mobile phone contracts)
- Support staff contacts required for operational areas such as networks, Wintel, virtualization, Unix, and database administrators
- Agency contacts and agreements and documenting resources that will be made available if support staff are not available

Final Thoughts

IT service continuity should work in harmony with business-continuity planning. Moreover, business-continuity planning should address what the business needs—not necessarily what the business wants.

When implementing effective IT service-continuity management, it is worth remembering the need versus the want. Many IT service-continuity management implementations are driven by wants; these implementations cost millions and deliver short of their expectations.

A final reflection on IT service-continuity management implementation: review, remediate, and maintain.

If you have any feedback or if you would like more information about IT service-continuity management, disaster-recovery planning, high availability, and business-continuity planning, email: info@itscm.com.au or visit www.itscm.com.au. Here you'll find support, tools, and templates related to IT service-continuity management, scheduling, and testing.